My Three Little Dots
on the
BIG WORLD MAP

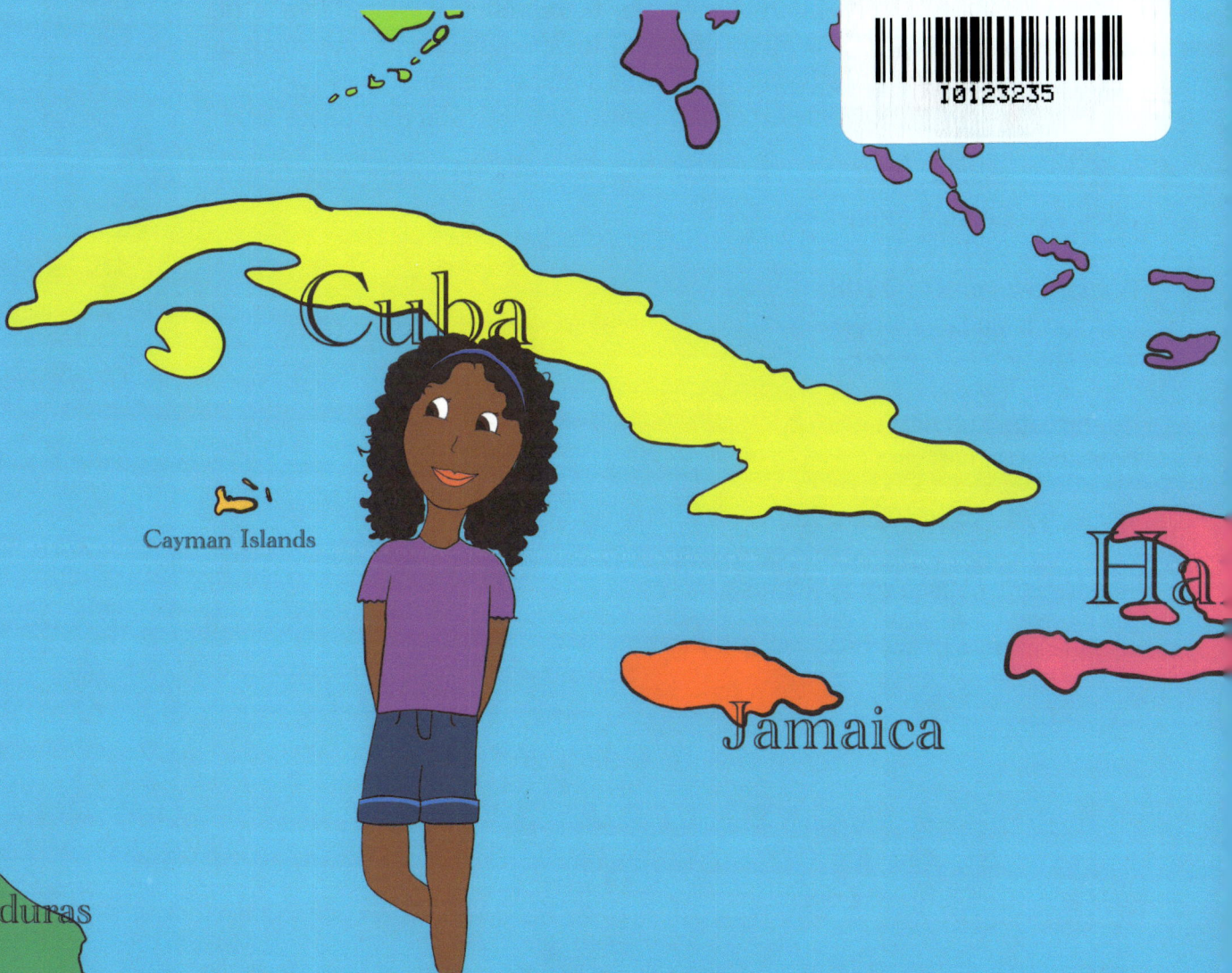

Cuba

Cayman Islands

Ha

Jamaica

onduras

EK JASMINE

CLMPublishing

Published by CLM Publishing
P.O. Box 1217,
Grand Cayman KY1-1108,
Cayman Islands
www.clmpublishing.com

Contact the author at:
booksbyjasmine@gmail.com

ISBN: 978-1-948074-28-5

Illustrated by Lashawntae Robinson

Printed in the United States of America.

Dedication

Every child who calls these
three little dots HOME.

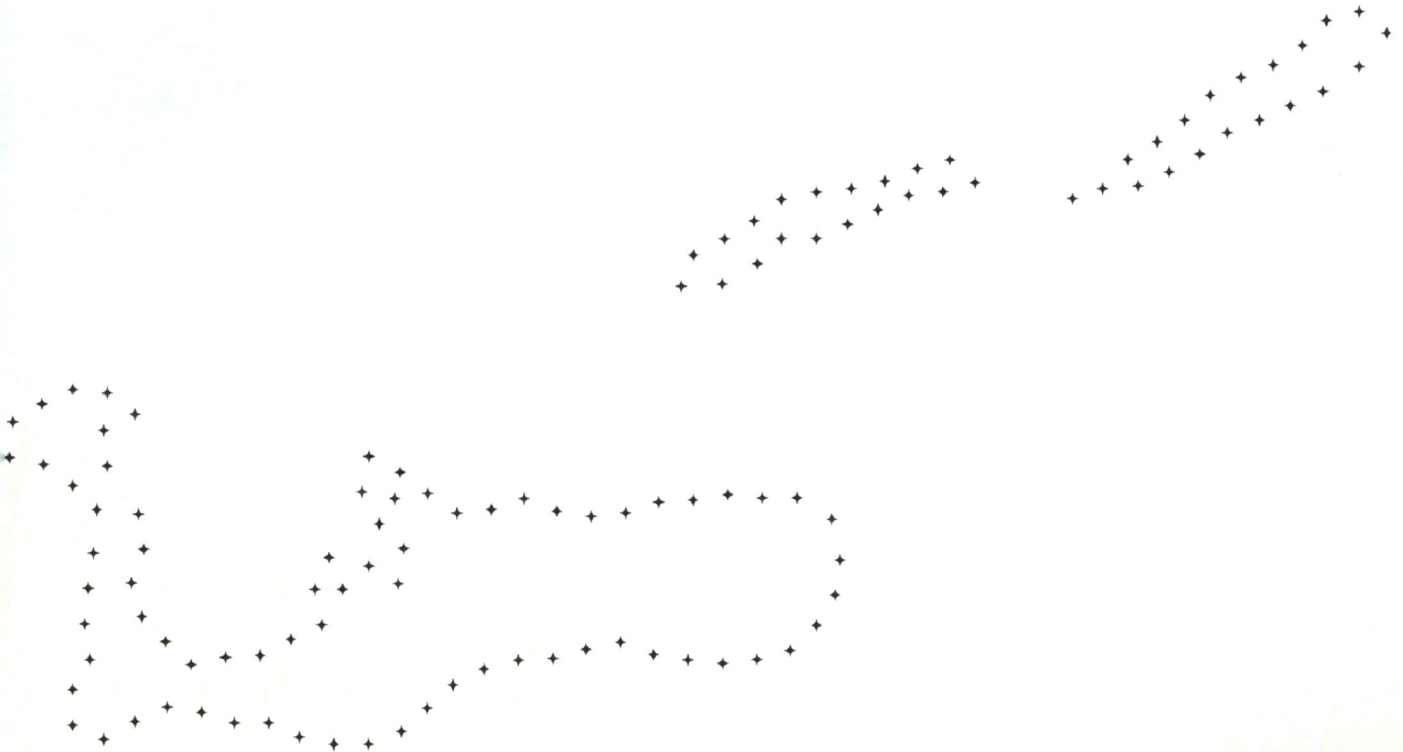

This book was made in part with a grant from the
Cayman National Cultural Foundation.

This is a true, true story
About my three little dots.
Making an enormous mark
Hooray! on the big world map.

Before one THOUSAND FIVE
HUNDRED and THREE,

Seems no one knew
'bout this marvellous place.

Then suddenly, yep,
we were DISCOVERED,

By an ITALIAN and his ship mates!

The More You Know ⭐

On August 3, 1492, Christopher Columbus and
his crew set sail from the port of Palos in southern
Spain on three vessels: la **Santa Clara (Niña)**,
la **Pinta**, and la **Santa Gallega (Santa Maria)**.
He made it to Las Tortugas, May 1503.

The EXPLORER CHRISTOPHER COLUMBUS
Sailed from a faraway country called SPAIN
And almost missed these three little dots;
As they are tiny, tiny, like grains.

A long, long, long, time ago,
These dots' names meant TURTLES.
But would've been funnier
If they were called URKELS.

Many, yes, many years later,
These three little dots' names were changed
From LAS TORTUGAS to CAYMAN ISLANDS
By a famous man called SIR FRANCIS DRAKE.

The More You Know ★

Sir Francis Drake changed the
names in 1586. The word *Caiman*
(Cayman) is Spanish for crocodiles.

The national flag consists of a blue ensign
It was adopted around nineteen fifty-nine

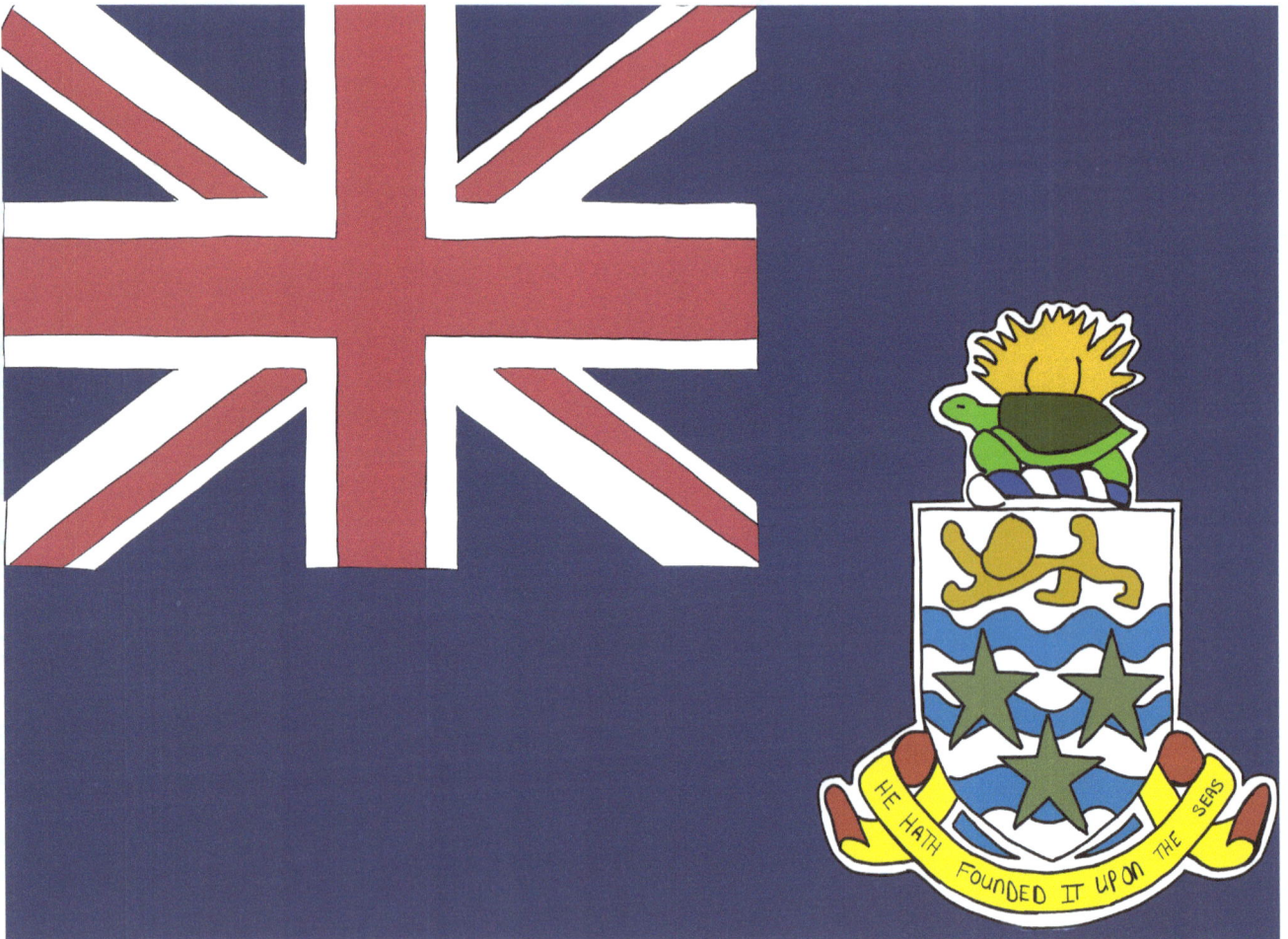

There are many things
That make up these little dots.
We're kind and friendly people,
Yes! But more than that.

Just know when you need to find us
Look for the Caribbean Sea
Near the Gulf of Mexico;
You will surely find these three.

The More You Know ⭐

The *biggest of the three dots* is Grand Cayman (22 miles long).
The *medium dot* is Cayman Brac (11.81 miles long).
The smallest one is Little Cayman (10 miles long).

Our history is connected
To several nearby islands,
Like HONDURAS and NICARAGUA,
And of course, CUBA'S ISLE OF PINE.

And when you search other data,
Guess what?! Close ties to JAMAICA.

Gulf of
Mexico

Fort Myers
USA
Fort Lauderdale
Miami

Straits of Florida

NASSAU

Andros

Great Bahama Bank

THE BAHAMAS

LA HABANA
Matanzas

Pinar del Río
CUBA
Santa Clara

Golfo de
Batabano
Nueva Gerona
Cienfuegos

Isla de la
Juventud
Ciego de Ávila

Camagüey

Las Tunas
Holguín

Golfo de
Guacanayabo
Bayamo

Santiago
de Cuba
Guantánamo

Guantanamo Bay
(US)

Cayman Islands

Windward Pass

JAMAICA
Jéré
Montego Bay

May Pen
KINGSTON
Spanish
Town

CARIBBEAN SEA

Many islands are much bigger
Way bigger than these *little* dots,
Which might make us look invisible,
But honestly, we are far from that.

ATLANTIC

OCEAN

Isla de Hispaniola
Cap-
Haïtien
Santiago de
los Caballeros
DOMINICAN
REPUBLIC
Gonaïves
ITI
San Juan de
la Maguana
San Pedro
de Macorís • Higüey
Mona Passage
San Juan
San Juan
T-AU-PRINCE
SANTO
DOMINGO
Ponce
Puerto
Rico

The Islands' National Bird
Is the GRAND CAYMAN PARROT,
It has five beautiful colours;
But no orange like a carrot.

The More You Know ⭐

The Grand Cayman Parrot is iridescent green with a white eye ring, red cheeks, black ear patches, and brilliant-blue wing feathers.

The SILVER THATCH PALM
Is the National Tree
You can make lovely things
From the leaves, while you sing!

Our DISCOVERY DAY
Is on the tenth of May.
Many records have shown
What our history says.

Ropes, brooms, and roofs can be made from the Silver Thatch Palm Tree.

The COAT OF ARMS with crested helm,
The motto, and a trademarked shield,
"He hath founded it upon the seas"
We stand with pride and solemnly read.

"BELOVED ISLE CAYMAN"
Is the National Song.
Learn the words and verses
So you can sing along.

The More You Know

The Bible verse that best represents the Cayman Islands' Christian heritage is Psalm 24:2.

"Beloved Isle Cayman" was written by the late Mrs. Leila Ross Shier in 1930.

The wild BANANA ORCHID
Is the National Flower.
Of the twenty-six species,
This orchid has the power.

Though tiny dots these islands may be,
The United Kingdom rules these three.

We are called a British Overseas Territory (2022).

GEORGE TOWN is our capital,
With buildings a hundred years old.
Some pirates tried to raid us
Searching for treasures like gold.

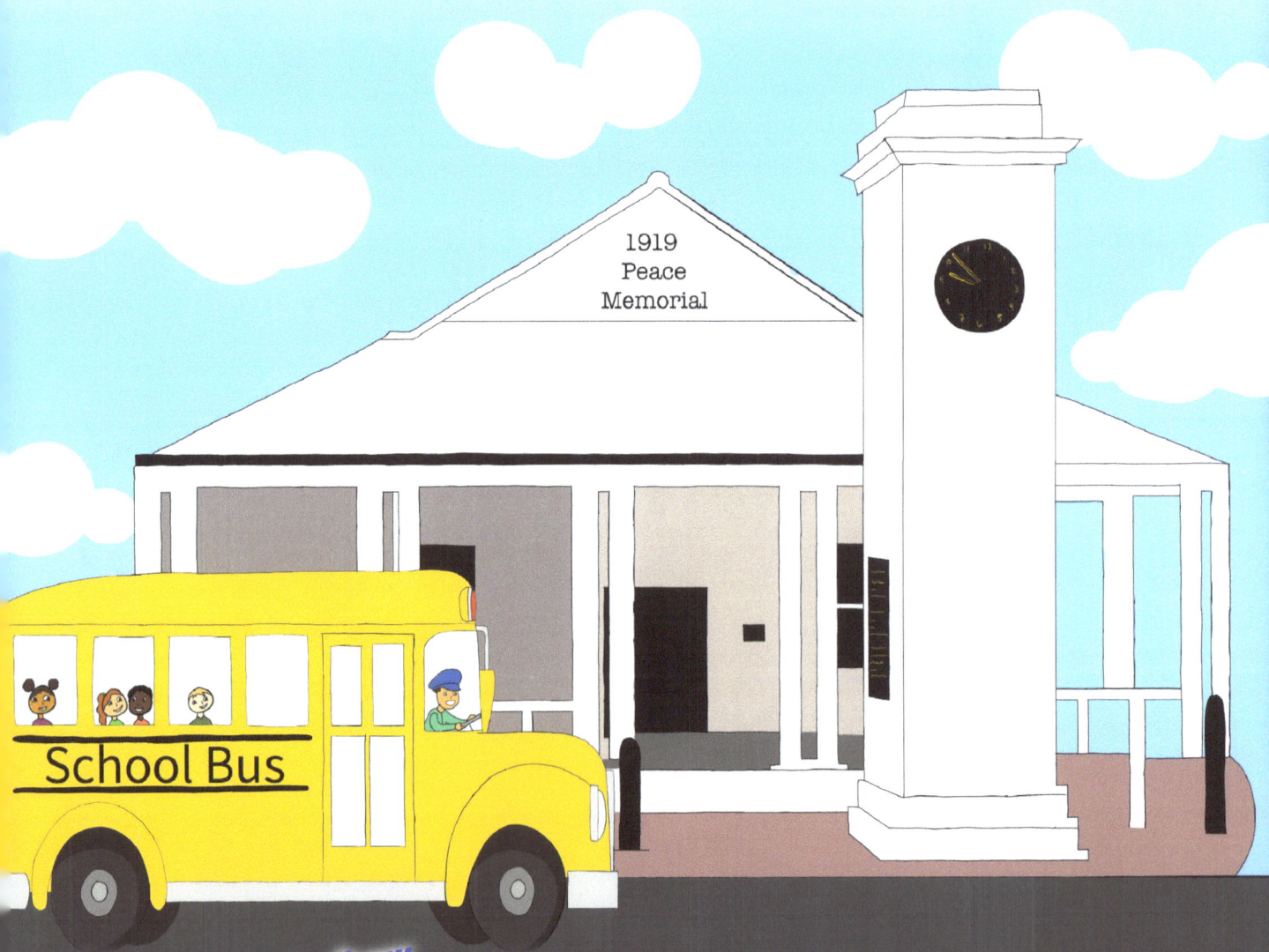

1919
Peace
Memorial

School Bus

The More You Know

The first capital was Bodden Town

This is a really cool place for family fun
You can swim with the stingrays, or soak up the sun
We have many nice places to hang out all day
Turtle Centre! Pedro Castle! Come out and play.

Little Cayman and Cayman Brac
Two of my famous little dots
Endorsed a relaxed and safe lifestyle,
Yes! your journey there will be worthwhile.

On these three little dots, you will find nice parks
And the National Trust provides nature walks
Then, try to relax on the Seven Mile stretch,
Or, at Botanic Park, you can take a rest.

TEN NATIONAL HEROES, now that is grand
They've made a difference to these islands.
Continue to look for folks to emulate
These three little dots are really doing great!

And now my Caymannites and foreigners, too
With heartfelt support, here is what you can do:
Lift hands in gratitude to the Creator
And pray we are safe in all kinds of weather.

Whether you look on a globe, an atlas, or on a large world map,
you will never again overlook these little dots.

For my three little dots' border protectors. Fill in the blanks.

1. What are the names of the three Cayman Islands?
   1) G _ _ _ _ _ C _ _ _ _ _ _
   2) C _ _ _ _ _ _ B _ _ _ _ _
   3) L _ _ _ _ _ _ C _ _ _ _ _

2. What famous Italian explorer visited these shores in 1503?
   1) C H R _ _ _ _ _ _ H _ R C _ _ _ _ _ _ S

3. Can you name the largest of the three Cayman Islands?
   1) G _ _ _ _ C _ _ _ _ _ _

4. Can you say when did Christopher Columbus discover these islands?

1) M _ _ 10, 15 _ _

5. What is the National Flower of these islands?

1) W _ L _   B _ N _ N _   O _ _ _ _ _ D

6. Do you know some products that can be made from the Silver Thatch Palm?

1) B _ O _ M

2) R O _ _

3) R _ _ F

7. What is the name of the islands I call my three little dots?

1) The C _ _ M _ N   I S _ _ _ _ _ S

8. What special day is May 10?

1) D _ S C _ V _ R _   D _ Y

9. What is the National Bird?

1) The Grand C _ Y M _ N P _ R R _ T

10. Who wrote the National Song?

1) LEIL _ _ R _ _ SS SHIE _ _

Answers

1. Grand Cayman. Cayman Brac. Little Cayman. **2.** Christopher Columbus. **3.** Grand Cayman.
4. May 10, 1503. **5.** Wild Banana Orchid. **6.** Broom. Rope. Roof. **7.** The Cayman Islands.
8. Discovery Day. **9.** The Grand Cayman Parrot. **10.** Leila Ross Shier.

National Song

(Leila Ross Shier) The Cayman Islands latest National Hero, 2022

1.

O land of soft, fresh breezes,
Of verdant trees so fair
With the Creator's glory reflected
ev'rywhere.
O sea of palest em'rald,
Merging to darkest blue,
When 'ere my thoughts fly Godward,
I always think of you.

Chorus:

Dear, verdant island, set
In blue Caribbean sea,
I'm coming, coming very soon,
O beauteous isle, to thee.
Although I've wandered far,
My heart enshrines thee yet.
Homeland! Fair Cayman Isle
I cannot thee forget.

The National Anthem

God Save the Queen
God save our gracious Queen!
Long live our noble Queen!
God save our Queen!
Send her victorious,
Happy and glorious,
Long to reign over us,
God save the Queen!

References

Page 10: https://en.wikipedia.org/wiki/Flag_of_the_Cayman_Islands

Page 11: https://www.britannica.com/place/Cayman-Islands

Page 14: www. Turtle.ky

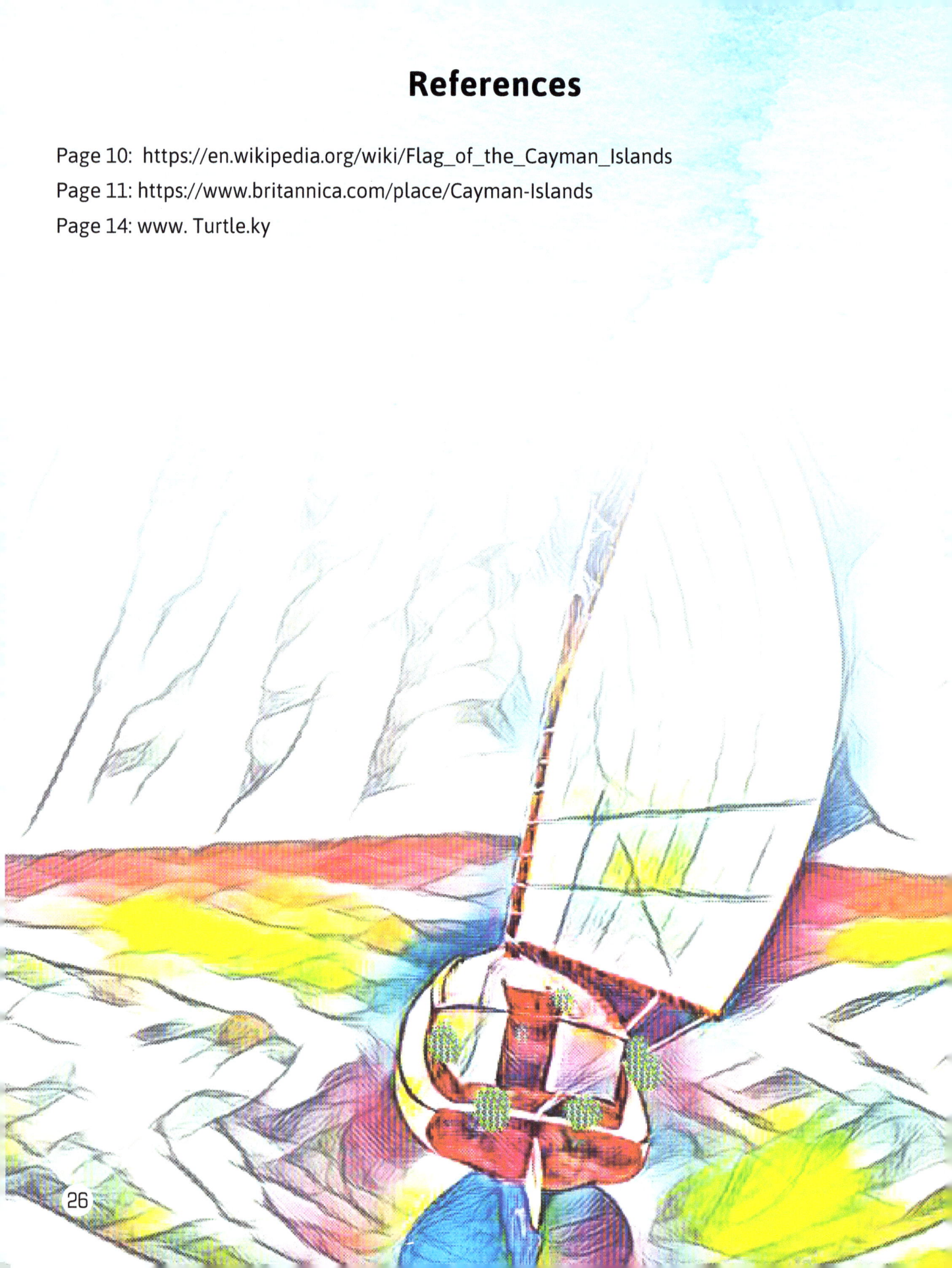